Roller Hockey

Roller Hockey

Mike Kennedy

Watts LIBRARY

Franklin Watts
A Division of Scholastic Inc.
New York • Toronto • London • Auckland • Sydney
Mexico City • New Delhi • Hong Kong
Danbury, Connecticut

Note to readers: Definitions for words in **bold** can be found in the Glossary at the back of this book.

Photographs ©: American Society of Mammalogists, Mammal Images Library: 32, 33 (J. D. Haweeli), 40, 41 (J. Visser); Animals Animals/Maresa Pryor: 35; B. Moose Peterson/WRP: 22, 23; BBC Natural History Unit: 21 (Niall Benvie), 37 (John Cancalosi), 5 bottom left, 5 top left (Brian Lightfoot), cover (Rico & Ruiz), 42 (Lynn Stone); Bruce Coleman: 24, 25 (R. Mittermeir), 31 (Han Reinhard); Corbis-Bettmann/George Lepp: 18, 19; Dembinsky Photo Assoc./John Gerlach: 27; NHPA/G.I. Bernard: 6; Peter Arnold Inc./C. Allan Morgan: 15; Photo Researchers, NY: 39 (G. C. Kelley), 7 (Maslowski), 1 (Rod Planck), 43 (Carroll Seghers); Visuals Unlimited: 13 (Gary W. Carter), 5 top right (John Gerlach), 5 bottom right (Gary Meszaros), 16, 17 (Tom J. Ulrich), 29 (Tom Walker).

The photo on the cover shows the opening face-off of a roller hockey game. The image opposite the title page shows a roller hockey game being played near the beach at sunset.

Library of Congress Cataloging-in-Publication Data

Kennedy, Mike (Mike William), 1965-
    Roller hockey / by Mike Kennedy.
        p. cm.—(Watts library)
    Includes bibliographical references and index.
    ISBN 0-531-13953-0 (lib. bdg.)   0-531-16583-3 (pbk.)
    1. Roller hockey—Juvenile literature. [1. Roller hockey.] I. Title. II. Series.

GV859.7 .K46 2001
796.21—dc21

00-043510

Contents

Children have played pick-up games of roller hockey for decades.

Chapter One

Rocking and Rolling

Who invented roller hockey? No one knows for sure. City kids back in the 1950s probably thought they did. And why not? In Boston, Chicago, Detroit, and New York, children loved to rumble on neighborhood streets in pick-up games of roller hockey. All they needed was a pair of **roller skates**, a hockey stick or a broom, and a homemade puck.

A good imagination also helped to make the games more exciting. Kids often pretended they were stars from the

This photograph was taken in the early 1900s at a roller-skating rink in New York City.

six National Hockey League teams. (That number has more than quadrupled since.) They dreamed about trading their roller skates for hockey skates and making it to the NHL. For most, the closest they would ever get were the streets outside their apartments. There, they played roller hockey until the Sun went down.

Were these spirited games the first versions of roller hockey? No. People had begun playing the sport about 80 years earlier. Roller hockey actually sprung from the country's fascination with roller-skating. It was only a few years after the first successful United States public roller rink opened in

Newport, Rhode Island in 1866 that children and adults discovered the thrill of roller hockey.

There is much more to this story, however. As you might guess, the sport is also a direct descendent of hockey. So, you might be wondering, just how did hockey and roller-skating come to be, and how did they meet to form roller hockey? The answers to these questions take us back hundreds of years.

Stick and Ball

When you think of hockey, you probably think of NHL stars such Paul Kariya or Jaromir Jagr firing a wicked **slap shot** in front of thousands of screaming fans. But this is not the way the game was played originally. The earliest forms of hockey were never intended for the ice. The sport was first contested on grassy fields by competitors using crude sticks to knock around a rock or ball. Hockey, in fact, is regarded as the oldest of all the stick-and-ball sports. This is one of the few things we know for sure about its origins.

We also know from an ancient carving that the people of Egypt enjoyed hockey as far back as 500 B.C. Further evidence suggests that other cultures throughout Africa, Asia, and Europe engaged in the sport, too. Two thousand years ago, children across the Roman Empire played hockey. Six hundred years ago, hockey became popular in France and Great Britain. Although different people in different places put different spins on the sport, one thing remained the same: hockey was played on grass. Unlike roller hockey, it was a slow game in which violent play and brute force were rewarded.

Things changed in the 1700s. People from cold-climate countries such as Holland, Scandinavia, and Canada discovered that hockey was much more exciting on a frozen pond or river. By this time, ice-skating had become quite common. It was just a matter of time before ice-skaters grabbed brooms and brought hockey to the ice. The ice added an entirely new dimension to the sport. Not only did the players move faster, so did the puck. This speedy new version of hockey developed into an extremely popular game, especially in Canada.

Roll With It

At about the same time, a man from Europe named Joseph Merlin was busy working on an innovation of his own. Joseph was a member of the Dutch Royal Academy of Sciences, as well as a maker of musical instruments. He also loved to ice-skate, but was out of luck in the summer as the layers of ice covering nearby ponds melted, leaving him nowhere to practice until winter came again. This gave Joseph an ingenious idea. One day in 1760, he attached wooden wheels in a straight line to the bottom of his shoes. He had invented the **inline skate**. (The roller skate, which features pairs of wheels positioned side-by-side, would not be invented for another 100 years.)

There was a problem, however. Joseph could not stop or turn on his skates, something he found out in the most unfor-

What's in a name?

Where did the term "hockey" come from? Some people believe that Native Americans developed it. The Micmac claim they invented hockey hundreds of years ago. The word also can be traced to the Iroquois, who played a game on ice with sticks and a ball. When a player got whacked with a stick or hit by the ball, he yelled, "Hogee!" This term means "It hurts!"

tunate of ways. Merlin planned to unveil his invention at a costume party in England, where he hoped to make a grand entrance. Playing one of his favorite songs on the violin, Joseph sped along on his skates into the beautiful ballroom where the masquerade was being held. Everyone in attendance was quite impressed—until Joseph crashed headfirst into a large and expensive mirror. The mirror and the violin shattered. Fortunately, though injured, Joseph remained in one piece.

Despite Joseph Merlin's clumsy introduction of the inline skate, the sport soon caught on. By the mid-1800s, inline skating had become a worldwide phenomenon. Other inventors continually improved on the original idea. The biggest breakthrough, the roller skate, came in 1863 from an American named James Leonard Plimpton. He called his model the "Rocket Skate," partly because its design made turning at high speeds much simpler. It also was easier to keep your balance on these skates. As a result, even more people began to roller-skate. As the number of skaters grew, variations of the sport popped up. This is how roller hockey was born.

James Leonard Plimpton invented the roller skate in 1863.

Going International

By the turn of the century, ice hockey was being played on both sides of the Atlantic. Naturally, roller-skating enthusiasts began to wonder: why not try the same thing on roller skates?

The new sport challenged their athletic skills and offered the speed they craved. History books say the first games actually were seen as early as 1870.

Though roller hockey was much different from ice hockey, people liked it just the same. Teams consisted of only five players, including the **goalie**. Pushing and checking were not allowed. Rules prevented the ball (which was used instead of a puck) from being lofted higher than six feet in the air.

In 1910, France hosted the first international roller hockey tournament. A British team called the Crystal Palace Engineers won the title and soon became famous worldwide, partly because of where they practiced. Back in London, the Engineers trained in the Crystal Palace, a magnificent structure made almost entirely of glass. Over the next three decades, Crystal Palace became the unofficial home of roller hockey, as British teams took one title after another. That all

The Crystal Palace, shown here, was home to the Crystal Palace Engineers, England's greatest roller hockey team.

changed during the 1940s. After World War II, countries such as Spain, Portugal, and Switzerland had improved greatly. Heading into the 1950s, the British no longer ruled the sport.

During the next several decades, roller hockey continued to spread around the world, but it paled in comparison to ice hockey, which most people viewed as more exciting. The action in ice hockey was fast and furious. Roller hockey, on the other hand, was much milder. Roller hockey players simply could not skate as fast as their counterparts on the ice. This was partly because roller hockey players used roller skates, not inline skates. If roller hockey was going to flourish, it required an injection of speed.

Getting Inline

The transformation roller hockey needed was sparked in a garage sale in Minnesota of all places, thanks to a pair of brothers who were crazy about ice hockey. In the spring of 1980, Scott and Brennan Olson were rummaging through a mountain of unwanted items at a neighbor's house when they spotted something very curious: an old pair of skates with four wheels lined up one after the other. Their eyes lit up when they saw the skates. They believed the inline "blades" would make a great off-season training device.

The origin of this pair of inline skates was a bit of a mystery. The skates could have been from a company that had patented a similar inline skate design in the 1960s. The skates also could have been one of the pairs given away by a popular

Viva, Las Vegas

Today, you do not have to cross the Atlantic to visit the Crystal Palace. A huge facility with the same name was built in Las Vegas in 1998. It hosts some of the most prestigious roller hockey tournaments in the world.

13

soft drink company in the 1970s. These models strapped on right over your sneakers. Scott and Brennan, however, did not care. Their only concern was whether the skates could take the pounding they were sure to give them. On further inspection, the brothers determined that they had to replace the wheels. They chose wheels that were made from a soft, rubbery material called **urethane**. It was a wise choice. Urethane wheels hugged the pavement and offered a smooth ride, making inline skating a breeze.

Scott and Brennan Olson started the company Rollerblade in their basement.

Scott and Brennan soon found that they loved designing inline skates almost as much as playing hockey. They started a company in their basement, naming it Rollerblade. Other inline skate companies followed, and the sport quickly developed into a national craze.

This was just what the doctor ordered for roller hockey, so to speak. Craving the speed and precision offered by urethane wheels, many players switched to the new Rollerblade models. This changed the very nature of roller hockey, as the sport became more fast-paced.

By the 1990s, roller hockey more closely resembled ice hockey. Professional leagues began to spring up everywhere. Roller Hockey International launched teams from coast to coast. Major League Roller Hockey created divisions for men and women. Pro Beach Hockey set up shop within a slap shot of the Pacific Ocean and added ramps behind the nets for the wildest version of the sport yet.

Amateur leagues also flourished. USA Hockey, the governing body of ice hockey and roller hockey in the U.S., created an inline hockey program in 1994. It currently sponsors leagues and tournaments nationwide. A variety of roller hockey programs are offered by USA Roller Sports, which operates under the command of the U.S. Olympic Committee. The North American Roller Hockey Championships were contested for the first time in 1994. The Pan American Games included roller hockey among its events in 1999. Today, roller hockey is as popular as Little League baseball, as thousands of kids play in leagues and just for fun.

The driveway is a great place to practice roller hockey.

Chapter Two

Rules of the Game

Want to know a perfect place to learn the game of roller hockey? Your driveway. This is where a lot of kids start. There, you can set up a goal and practice. Working on the game's fundamentals is important, especially for beginners. Before you are ready for live action, you have to get comfortable on your inline skates and pick up the basics of stickhandling, passing, and shooting. Since space is limited in your driveway, it is easier to concentrate on specific skills.

Of course, the sport is played somewhat differently when you get into real competition. Leagues and tournaments are governed by official rules. Games are divided into two periods—usually between 15 and 25 minutes each—and the rink must be a certain size. The rules for USA Hockey say a roller hockey rink must be between 145 and 185 feet (44.2 and 56.4 meters) long (nearly twice the size of an NBA court), and from

A roller hockey rink is longer than it is wide.

65 to 85 feet (20 to 26 meters) wide. The center red line divides the rink in half. There are also rules governing the playing surface. It must be made of wood, cement, plastic, or asphalt. In addition, a wall or fence (known as the **boards**) must surround the playing surface. Players are free to roam in either end without the puck or ball. Imagine all the room that gives you! This is why the fastest skaters and the best stick-handlers and passers flourish in roller hockey.

What's Your Position?

Here is a tricky question. Five players from each team are allowed to play at the same time, but how many positions are there? The answer is three: **forward** (2), **defense** (2), and goalie. Each has different responsibilities.

Forwards provide a team's scoring. To excel at this position, you need an accurate shot and pinpoint passing skills. Forwards spend their time zipping up and down the length of the rink. They are constantly on the lookout for a chance to break free in the **attacking zone** and score a goal. Forwards also have to help out on defense. Obviously, this position is hard to master if you are not in great shape.

On defense, the main responsibility is limiting the scoring chances of opposing forwards by stealing passes and deflecting shots. Playing defense requires quick hands and good in-stincts. You also must develop top-notch skating skills. Defensemen often have to start and stop quickly, and skate backwards. While you don't have to be fast, you must

In the game above, the team in white is playing defense. You can see one of the defenders (number 22) deflecting a shot.

anticipate an opponent's every move. Once defensemen take care of business in their own end, they are free to skate out of the **defensive zone** to help the offensive players.

Goalie is the only position with no offensive responsibilities. The main job is to stop shots from going in the net.

Quick-Change Artists

When forwards and defensemen get tired, teammates on the bench replace them. Sometimes, these changes are made on the fly, which means the action does not stop. Goalies do not have this luxury, however. Unless there is an injury or a team decides it needs an extra forward, the goalie never leaves the playing surface.

Lightning-quick reflexes and a cool head are a goalie's best friends. There is no time to panic when an opposing forward winds up for a shot. You need to concentrate on the puck or ball, and judge its speed and direction the instant it leaves the shooter's stick. When you stop a shot, you have to control the puck or ball and keep it away from opposing forwards. Well-trained goalies hardly ever give up a rebound. These "second-chance" shots are often the easiest way for an opponent to score.

Check That

Roller hockey at its best is fast and exciting with non-stop action. If you turn your head for even a second, you might miss a goal. How is the game able to maintain such a break-neck pace? Rules are in place to let players move up and down the rink without being bumped or slammed into the boards.

The "no body checking" rule, in fact, is the most important rule in roller hockey. This separates the sport from ice hockey, where bruising hip checks and shoulder blows are part of the game. Roller hockey, however, thrives on speed. Free from the threat of being checked, players can try daring moves at top speed. Roller hockey does not have **offsides** and **icing** rules,

Body checking is not allowed in roller hockey.

either. These rules prevent ice hockey skaters from staying in the offensive zone while their teammates play defense in their own end.

The rest of roller hockey's rules are similar to those of ice hockey. For example, you are not allowed to carry your stick above your shoulders, or use it to hook, trip, slash, or spear an opponent. You can, however, hit another player's stick with yours. Fighting is against the regulations, too. Elbowing and other unnecessary rough play are also forbidden.

The referee is in charge of enforcing the rules. No contest can start until he drops the puck for the opening **face-off**. If the referee spots someone breaking the rules, he sends the guilty party to the **penalty box**. The penalty box is where offenders "serve their time." Penalties can range from two minutes for minor infractions to outright ejections for major violations. When you go to the "box," you cannot return until

A roller hockey game officially starts when the referee drops the puck for the opening face-off.

your penalty time expires or the opposition scores. This leaves your team **short-handed** and gives the other team a **power play**. In other words, your squad skates with one less player, while your opponent is allowed to continue with the normal number of players.

Win, Lose, or Tie

The object of roller hockey is to score more goals than your opponent. A goal is credited when the ball or puck completely crosses the **goal line** running across the mouth of the net. If even the smallest fraction of the ball or puck is resting on that line, it is not considered a goal. Goals are scored often during a power play by the team with the extra skater. It is a simple math equation. The short-handed team does not have enough

players to guard each opposing player. This usually leaves someone open for a good scoring attempt. In fact, teams practice specific plays to take advantage of this situation.

Sometimes neither team outscores the other. In this case, the game is declared a tie. Roller hockey is one of few sports that allows such an outcome. Of course, there are occasions when a winner must be determined. If teams are tied after reg-

ulation in the finals of a tournament, they play a five-minute "sudden death" **overtime** (OT) period. In OT, the team that scores first wins. If no one puts the puck in the net, then a **shoot-out** follows. During the shoot-out, four players from each team get a free shot at the goalie with no defense in the way. It is the ultimate one-on-one challenge. The team that scores the most goals during the shoot-out wins.

A goal is scored when the entire puck or ball crosses the goal line.

*Roller hockey can be
a fast-paced sport.*

Chapter Three

Suiting Up for Speed

Why is roller hockey so exciting? One word says it all: speed. The sport is custom-made for skaters who love to race up and down the rink. How are they able to skate so rapidly? Equipment has a lot to do with it. For example, many companies design skates specifically for roller hockey. World-class players rocket around the rink on these inline models, stop on a dime, and change direction in a flash.

There is a potential downside to the speedy world of roller hockey, however.

The chance for injury is great when a player is not properly equipped. Falling, especially on concrete or asphalt, can really hurt. If you get hit by the puck or ball, it can sting. That is why smart roller hockey players never start a game or practice without wearing all necessary protective gear. Those who are well prepared have little to worry about once they enter the action.

Skate Debate

What is the most important piece of equipment in roller hockey? Skates, of course. Obviously, choosing the right pair requires plenty of thought and research. If you already own roller hockey skates, you know that a huge selection is available. Dozens of companies offer a variety of models featuring all sorts of new technology designed specifically for roller hockey. Some of the leading manufacturers are Bauer, CCM, Easton, Koho, Mission, and V-Formation. These companies sell models that look very similar to ice hockey skates.

Roller hockey skates lace up like basketball sneakers. They have four narrow wheels that simulate the blade of an ice

Safety First

Many experts advise players just learning to skate to start with a pair of inline skates, which are different from the ones used in roller hockey. Inline skates provide sturdy support around the ankle. They also have brakes. These features make it easier to keep your balance and stop. Eventually, you can try roller hockey skates.

hockey skate. Often, the first and last wheels are **rockered**. This means they are raised slightly off the ground. Rockered wheels allow experienced skaters to make sharp turns at top speeds.

Roller hockey skates lace up and tie just like a pair of high-top sneakers.

Stick With It

Roller hockey sticks are almost exactly like ice hockey sticks. This was not always the case, however. For many years, players used shorter, more rigid models shaped like candy canes. It was not until the 1970s that ice hockey sticks became standard issue.

Today, of course, the situation is different. It is difficult to distinguish a roller hockey stick from an ice hockey stick. Both are constructed from lightweight materials such as wood, **graphite**, or **aluminum**, which give shooters maximum

power. Rules governing a stick's **shaft**, the long, straight part of the stick, and **blade** do exist, however. In roller hockey, no shaft can extend longer than 60 inches (152.4 centimeters) from its top to its **heel**. The blade (the curved part of the stick at the bottom) must be between 2 and 3 inches (5.1 and 7.6 cm) wide. Within these guidelines, players modify their sticks to suit their needs. For example, some prefer a big curve in the blade. This type of blade benefits players who have a wicked **wrist shot** because they are able to cradle the puck or ball and whip it faster at the goal.

Thanks to lightweight sticks, players can easily control the puck or ball.

Protect Yourself

Injuries are a part of any sport, and roller hockey is no exception. There are steps you can take, however, to lessen the likelihood of injuries and their seriousness. The first is to wear a hockey helmet with a chin strap. If you are under age 18, your helmet must have a full facemask. All players, from beginners to pros, must use a mouthguard, as well. The helmet, facemask, and mouthguard offer protection from hard shots and sticks raised above shoulder level.

The rules also state that players must be outfitted with elbow pads and hockey gloves on their arms and hands. Since roller hockey prohibits body checking, shoulder pads and hip pads are unnecessary. Knee and shin protectors, however, are mandatory, and will save you from bumps, bruises, and scrapes. Hockey pants are a wise investment, too. This is especially true if you play defense. Blocking shots takes equal parts of skill and guts, and you will become much better at it if the sting of the puck or ball is not a concern.

Goalie Gear

Any goalie will tell you that kicking away a slap shot or gloving a wrist shot takes more than quick feet and hands. Netminders, or goalies, rely on special padding and equipment to help them do their job. One of the keys to being a good goalie is seeing the puck or ball. This is why a mask is so important.

It is important to wear a helmet with a chin strap and a full face mask.

Choose one that provides a full view of the playing surface and fully protects your head. Don't worry about how cool or stylish your mask looks. Goalies look their best when they are making great saves.

Another crucial piece of equipment is the goalie stick, which is much different than a regular stick. About halfway down the shaft and all the way through the blade, a goalie stick gets very wide. This design helps netminders in several ways. The extra bulk makes the stick more sturdy, so the chances of it breaking on a hard shot are slim. The odd shape of the goalie stick also comes into play during scrambles in front of the net. Goalies often lay their sticks flat on the ground to stop rebound shots.

Goalies wear large, soft pads on their hands and legs, as well as on their shoulders and chest, to absorb the impact of high-speed shots. The **blocker**, which some people call the "waffle" because of its size and shape, goes on your stick hand. The **catcher**, or catching glove, goes on the other hand. Similar to a first baseman's mitt in baseball, it is used to snatch

Standing Tall

Straightaway skating speed is not the key to good goaltending. Developing quick lateral movement and alert reflexes, on the other hand, is essential. You must be able to move instantly from one side of the goal mouth to the other. "Playing the angles" is equally important. Don't position yourself in the center of the **goal crease**. It is better to challenge shooters by coming out of the net and making their shots more difficult.

Goalies wear a lot of protective equipment. Besides a helmet, they are outfitted with pads on their legs, shoulders, and chest as well as a blocker on one hand and a catching glove on the other.

shots out of mid-air. Moving with all this "armor" covering your body is not easy. With patience and practice, however, you will become comfortable in your gear. It also helps to do a lot of stretching before you play to keep your body flexible and nimble.

Professional roller hockey has not found its audience yet, but it still may hit the big time.

Chapter Four

Pro-files

Is it possible to earn a living playing roller hockey? Certainly. Is it easy to earn a living playing roller hockey? Certainly not. Since the early 1990s, professional leagues have started all across North America. Most have gone out of business. Unfortunately, professional roller hockey has not caught on like ice hockey and other major sports. In fact, there are diehard NHL supporters who don't give roller hockey much of a look, even though they would probably love the sport.

Professional roller hockey players make little money. They play because they love the sport or because they dream of being discovered by an NHL team. Eric Messier is a good example. Eric has carved out a successful NHL career, but he got his start in 1995 with the Montreal Roadrunners of Roller Hockey International (RHI). Among today's NHL players, Eric probably owes the most to roller hockey, but he is not the only one who has benefited from the sport.

Brotherly Love

The two most famous products of roller hockey happen to be brothers: Brian and Joey Mullen. They starred in the NHL in the 1980s and 1990s, combining for 762 goals, a total that would make any pair of pros proud. Joey, who accounted for more than 500 of them, also played for three Stanley Cup championships. None of this would have been possible without roller hockey.

Brian and Joey grew up in the 1970s in a rough section of New York City called Hell's Kitchen. Their father, Tom, and John, their uncle, passed on to them a passion for hockey. The only problem was that the nearest usable ice hockey rink was miles away across the Hudson River. Brian and Joey instead turned to roller hockey, playing on the streets and in schoolyard leagues in their neighborhood. "Roller hockey was the national sport of our neighborhood," recalls Brian. "We grew up on roller skates. You'd be surprised what you can do on them."

The Mullen brothers could do almost anything on their skates, which was crucial in the rough and tumble games contested in Hell's Kitchen. Roller hockey there was far different than the current version of the sport. Tempers ran high during games. Punishing checks and dirty play were an accepted part of the action. Since neither Brian nor Joey was very big, each had to learn to play with intelligence. It was the best way to excel and the only way to survive.

Joey Mullen of the Pittsburgh Penguins, left, celebrates after a goal in a game against the Florida Panthers.

Brian Mullen, right, battles for position during a game in 1989 against the Philadelphia Flyers.

Eventually, both took to the ice, where their careers soared. Each earned an ice hockey **scholarship**— Joey to Boston College and Brian to the University of Wisconsin. The St. Louis Blues drafted Joey in 1979. Brian was picked by the Winnipeg Jets in 1982. Several years later, Brian and Joey made headlines when each earned a spot in the 1989 All-Star game.

"God gave them the talent, and they were seen by the right people over the years," the boys' mother, Marion, once said. "But they earned this for themselves, and they both deserve it." As Brian and Joey will tell you, the sport of roller hockey, which helped pave their way to NHL stardom, deserves some credit as well.

Oh, Brother

What do Chris Chelios, Marty McSorley, Joe Sakic, and Brett Hull have in common? True, all have logged more than 10 years in the NHL, but did you also know that each has a brother who either played or coached in RHI? Steve Chelios, Chris McSorley, and Brian Sakic all have suited up for RHI teams at one time or another. Bobby Hull, Jr. was coach of the Los Angeles Blades in 1996.

Sister Act

Speaking of siblings, a number of celebrated sisters have also made their mark in roller hockey. A goalie named Manon Rheaume, whose younger brother, Pascal, is a **winger** for the St. Louis Blues, was arguably the best ever to play professionally. She was the first woman to play for an NHL team when she appeared in a preseason game in 1992. She also broke barriers in professional roller hockey when she played goalie for the New Jersey Rockin' Rollers and the Sacramento River Rats in the mid-1990s. "It's never been easy," Manon says. "But I've always wanted to play hockey. I'd rather play hockey than do anything else."

Manon developed her love for the sport growing up in Canada. She began ice-skating at age 3. Two years later, she found a home in goal as a netminder. She practiced constantly with her brothers, who fired one shot after another at her. Finding girls to compete against was much more difficult, however. When Manon turned 11, she became the first girl to play in a prestigious international ice hockey tournament held in Quebec.

That was just the beginning for Manon. In 1991, she joined a men's

Manon Rheaume is a hero to boys and girls everywhere who play roller hockey.

Family Affair

Hockey is a way of life in the Granato family. Tony, a former NHL All-Star, is probably the most famous of his brothers and sisters. Two younger siblings, Robbie and Cammi, have made their mark, too. Both have played in RHI. In fact, Cammi (pictured above right) was drafted by the Buffalo Wings in 1998, just months after she had led the U.S. women's ice hockey team to a gold medal at the Winter Olympics in Nagano, Japan.

junior hockey team called the Trois-Rivieres Draveurs, becoming the first woman to reach this level. A year later, using this experience to her advantage, she led Canada to the title in the women's World Championship. Manon and her teammates repeated as champs in 1994, and she was named the tournament's Most Valuable Player for the second time in a row.

Manon's success on the ice ultimately took her to the roller rink, as New Jersey signed her in 1994 after the women's World Championship. In one contest in her first season with the Rockin' Rollers, her team beat the Pittsburgh Phantoms in front of 12,000 screaming fans at the Meadowlands. The game was most notable, however, because Erin Whitten opposed New Jersey as the goalie for Pittsburgh. It marked the first time two women had faced each other in a men's professional league.

After two years with the Rockin' Rollers, Manon was traded to Sacramento, where she continued to blaze new trails. In the summer of 1996, she became the first female goalie in RHI history to record a win against a team with a male goalie when her River Rats beat the San Diego Barracudas, 12–10. "My goal is just to go farther than where I thought I could," she says. "If you

Manon Rheaume stands tall in goal for the Sacramento River Rats.

Out-Whitted

If Manon Rheaume is the best female goalie ever, Erin Whitten is not far behind her. Erin was an All American on the women's ice hockey team at the University of New Hampshire in the late 1980s. After college, Erin became the first U.S. woman to suit up for an NHL affiliate when she skated for the Adirondack Red Wings, Detroit's team in the American Hockey League. In RHI, she was a member of the Oakland Skates and the Pittsburgh Phantoms. Erin's biggest thrill came on the ice, however. She was goalie when the U.S. women took ice-hockey gold at the '98 Winter Olympics.

have that kind of desire, I think you can achieve what you want to achieve."

Szenszational

Tony Szabo has a similar attitude to Manon, and it has served him well. Many people regard him as the Wayne Gretzky of roller hockey. "I started playing roller hockey when most people did not take it very seriously," he says. "But now, anyone can see how roller hockey has impacted my life."

Tony, who was born in Flint, Michigan in 1968, grew up playing ice hockey. From an early age, he had great coordination, and was strong and fast. As a child, Tony played for an amateur ice hockey team called the Detroit Little Caesars. Scouts noticed his talent right away. He moved to Canada to play junior hockey as a teenager, and college coaches soon came knocking on his door. In 1990, Tony accepted a scholarship to Northern Michigan University. The freshman was named Rookie of the Year, and also helped NMU capture the NCAA championship.

Tony Szabo has skated into the record books during his roller hockey career.

Tony Szabo was all smiles after joining Pro Beach Hockey's Web Warriors.

Tony got married a few years later. He and his wife, Kristi, then embarked on a journey that took them all over the globe. Tony played for ice hockey teams in Italy, Sweden, and Scotland. At one point, he returned to North America to try out for the Ottawa Senators of the NHL.

Tony came back to the U.S. for good in 1994. The second RHI season was about to begin, and the Atlanta Fire Ants wanted the high-scoring forward. The following season, he joined the Detroit Motor City Mustangs, led the league in goals with 50, and was selected Player of the Year. In 1996, while playing for the Long Island Jawz, Tony lit the lamp for six goals during the All-Star game. Two years later, RHI suspended play for a season because of financial problems. No problem. Tony immediately became captain of the Web Warriors, one of Pro Beach Hockey's best teams.

In 1999, Tony claimed his first RHI title. With the league back in business, he suited up for the St. Louis Vipers. The team finished first in the Eastern Conference and faced off against the Anaheim Bullfrogs in a one-game, winner-take-all final. Late in the first half, Tony scored a crucial goal to put St. Louis up by one. The Vipers held on for a hard-fought victory by a score of 8 to 6. "Playing on this team was probably the best 'team' experience in all my years with RHI," he says.

Today, Tony continues to nurture the sport that has given him so much. Among other things, he serves as Vice President of Hockey Operations for a roller hockey company called V-Formation. Tony is very eager to see the rise of new professional leagues. "There aren't many people who have been able to advance in the field of his or her choice," he says proudly. "It's a great game."

Precious Time

Like many professional roller hockey players, Tony Szabo can crank a slap shot at more than 70 miles per hour. If he fires a puck just as he crosses the center red line, how much time does the goalie have to react? Not much. If you do the math, it comes out to less than one second.

Roller hockey continues to grow, with new generations of roller hockey players participating in inline programs each year.

Chapter Five

Overtime

Even though professional roller hockey leagues have struggled to stay in business, the sport in general is very healthy and has a bright future. In fact, all signs indicate that roller hockey's popularity is on the rise. Statistics show that participation in the sport has grown by more than 20 percent since the late 1980s, and that number should increase in the years to come. Thousands of kids and adults enroll in USA Hockey's inline program every year. Most of these members are under age 17, which means a new generation of roller hockey enthusiasts is emerging.

Tourney Time

NHL Breakout sponsors roller hockey tournaments in cities across the U.S. Each year, in fact, the tour concludes with national championship games for different age groups.

Breaking Out

The NHL is aware of roller hockey's growth. In fact, in recent years the league has discovered that the sport is crucial to ice hockey's development. The NHL believes that people who play roller hockey will naturally become interested in ice hockey, which has a lot to do with how the league has expanded. Today, the NHL is home to teams in Arizona, California, Florida, Georgia, Tennessee, and Texas. This is a radical departure from the old days when the NHL set up shop only in northern cities. Why is this significant? The NHL has helped introduce ice hockey and roller hockey to thousands of new fans. For most of the year in Southern states, the weather is warm and beautiful, which makes outdoor ice surfaces nearly impossible to find. What are NHL fans to do if they want to play hockey? Many strap on a pair of inline skates and head to a park for a game of roller hockey.

48

This team celebrates after an NHL Breakout event in California.

Great Expectations

Hockey legend Wayne Gretzky, whose nickname is the Great One, wants to see roller hockey flour- ish. To make sure it does, he is opening his own roller hockey centers nationwide.

This is partly why the league created a program called NHL Breakout. Every spring, summer, and fall, NHL Breakout visits cities all over North America. It is like a big carnival with fun activities and exciting games. Many of the events test your roller hockey skills. You can put on goalie gear and try your luck between the pipes, or you can see how your slap shot rates against the NHL's best. In addition, many of the league's top players help out with the program. Sometimes, stars such as Mike Modano or Martin Brodeur show up to sign autographs or offer playing tips.

Break Away

NHL Breakout is just one way to become more familiar with roller hockey. The sport is catching on in all corners of North America, as local youth leagues have become commonplace, both in the U.S. and Canada.

Though roller hockey has been around for more than 100 years, in many ways it is still taking its baby steps. Every year, people of all ages discover the sport and fall in love with it almost immediately. This is great news for young players, because you can become part of the generation that brings the sport to the next level. By joining the millions who already play, you can help roller hockey score big.

Timeline

500 B.C.	The Egyptians play an early form of hockey.
1400	Hockey's popularity begins to grow in Europe.
1700	Hockey moves to the ice in countries with cold climates in the Northern Hemisphere.
1760	An instrument maker named Joseph Merlin invents the inline skate in Europe.
1863	J.L. Plimpton invents the roller skate in the United States.
1870	The first games of roller hockey are played in Europe.
1910	The first international roller hockey tournament is held in France and won by Britain's Crystal Palace Engineers.
1940	International play is suspended because of World War II.
1947	International play resumes.
1963	A new inline skate is introduced in the United States, but generates little interest.
1980	The Olson brothers found Rollerblade. Other inline skate companies soon follow.
1993	Roller Hockey International debuts.
1994	USA Hockey creates a separate division for roller hockey. The North American Roller Hockey Championships debut.
1998	Pro Beach Hockey debuts.
1999	The Pan American Games, held in Canada, include roller hockey as an event for the first time.

Glossary

aluminum—a metallic substance used to make the shafts of hockey sticks.

attacking zone—the area that extends from the center red line to behind the opposition's net. The team with control of the puck or ball tries to move into the attacking zone to score a goal.

blade—the part of the hockey stick that extends horizontally from the bottom of the shaft.

blocker—the piece of equipment a goalie wears to protect his stick hand. Waffle is another term.

boards—the wood and glass barrier that surrounds and encloses the playing surface.

catcher—the glove goalies use to catch the puck or ball.

defense—a position in roller hockey. When playing defense, you are responsible for preventing the other team from scoring.

defensive zone—the area that extends from the center red line to behind your team's net.

face-off—the way in which the puck or ball is put into play. In a face-off, two opposing players face each other with their sticks forward. The referee drops the puck or ball between them.

forward—a position in roller hockey. The forward's top responsibility is to score goals.

goal crease—the small area in front of the net designated strictly for the goalie. Players are not allowed to interfere with the goalie in this space.

goal line—the line that runs across the mouth of the net. A goal is scored when the entire puck or ball crosses this line.

goalie—a position in roller hockey. The goalie's top responsibility is to stop the puck or ball from going in the net.

graphite—a material derived from carbon used to make the shafts of hockey sticks.

heel—the part of the stick where the shaft joins the blade.

icing—an infraction in ice hockey, but not in roller hockey. It occurs when the puck is shot from your side of the red line to a designated area in the opponent's end. The result of icing is a face-off back in your end.

inline skate—a skate with wheels aligned in a straight line.

offsides—an infraction in ice hockey, but not in roller hockey. It occurs when you precede the puck across the opponent's blue line. The result is a face-off outside the opponent's end of the ice.

overtime—a five-minute period played after regulation time expires in a roller hockey game when the score is tied. It is called "sudden death" because the team that scores first wins the game.

penalty box—the bench area along the boards where a player must sit during penalty time.

power play—a term used during penalty time. The team with more players on the playing surface is on the power play.

rockered—when the front and back wheels of an inline skate are slightly off the ground.

roller skates—skates with two, side-by-side pairs of wheels.

scholarship—when a college pays for a student's education. Scholarships can be awarded for athletics and academics.

shaft—the long part of the stick that extends vertically from the blade.

shoot-out—the process of determining the winning team in roller hockey when overtime expires without either team scoring.

short-handed—a term used during penalty time. The team with fewer players on the playing surface is short-handed.

slap shot—a shot in which the player takes a full wind-up to shoot the puck or ball.

urethane—the rubber-like material used to make the wheels of inline skates.

winger—a term for someone who plays either left wing or right wing in ice hockey.

wrist shot—a shot in which the player uses only his wrists. It is also called a "wrister."

To Find Out More

Books

Christopher, Matt. *Roller Hockey Radicals*. Little, Brown & Company, 1998.

Easter, David. *Winning Roller Hockey: Techniques, Tactics, Training*. Human Kinetics Publishing, 1997.

Gutman, Bill. *Roller Hockey*. Minneapolis, Capstone Press, 1995.

Millar, Cam. *Roller Hockey*. New York, Sterling Publishing Co., Inc., 1996.

Siller, Greg. *Roller Hockey: Skills and Strategies for Winning on Wheels*. Masters Press, 1997.

Werner, Doug. *In-Line Skater's Start-Up: A Beginner's Guide to In-Line Skating and Roller Hockey*. Tracks Publishing, 1995.

Organizations and Online Sites

Hockey Books

http://www.hockeybooks.com

Site that provides an extensive list of books about hockey, including many about roller hockey.

Inline Hockey

http://www.inlinehockey.net

Comprehensive site that provides all sorts of information on roller hockey, including updates on high school and college leagues, product news, and a book store.

Inline Hockey Central

http://www.inlinehockeycentral.com

Helpful site that offers everything from playing tips to late-breaking news on amateur and professional leagues.

Major League Roller Hockey

http://www.mlrh.com

Official site. Includes news updates and a rundown of men's and women's divisions.

NHL Breakout

http://www.nhl.com

Official site of the National Hockey League. Includes complete information on the NHL Breakout program.

North American Roller Hockey Championships

http://www.narch.com

Official site. Includes information on tournament schedules and results.

Roller Hockey Central

http://www.rollerhockeycentral.com

In-depth site that includes news on European leagues and a long list of links.

USA Hockey InLine

http://www.usahockey.com

Official site. Includes information on leagues, rules, equipment, and much more.

USA Roller Sports

http://www.usarollerskating.com

Official site. Includes information on U.S. national teams, as well as clinics and leagues.

A Note on Sources

In researching this book, I tried to draw on as many sources as possible. First, I consulted with another author named Mark Stewart. He knows a lot about sports, and runs his own company called Team Stewart. Mark pointed me in a couple different directions.

Then, I visited my local library and searched its database for books written about roller hockey. Two were very helpful—one was by Cam Millar and the other by Bill Gutman. There was another book called *The Young Inline Skater* by Chris Edwards that provided valuable assistance, too. In addition, a periodical known as *The Hockey News* runs a special section on roller hockey every year.

Finally, I searched the Internet. There, I discovered scores of great sites, including those sponsored by USA Hockey and USA Roller Sports. Obviously, the Internet is a terrific source of information on just about any subject.

—Mike Kennedy

Index

Numbers in *italics* indicate illustrations.

About the Author

Mike Kennedy is a freelance sportswriter whose work has ranged from Super Bowl coverage to historical research and analysis. He has profiled athletes in virtually every sport, including Peyton Manning, Bernie Williams, and Allen Iverson. He is a graduate of Franklin & Marshall College.

Mike has contributed his expertise to other books by Grolier, such as *Auto Racing: A History of Fast Cars and Fearless Drivers*. The other books he authored in this series are *Skateboarding* and *Soccer*.

Kids are playing roller hockey all over the country. This book introduces young readers to roller hockey's history, rules, positions, gear, and some of its professional players.

Watts LIBRARY

books about sports

Caving
Exploring Limestone Caves
By Larry Dane Brimner

Skateboarding
By Mike Kennedy

Soccer
By Mike Kennedy

ISBN 0-531-16583-3

9 780531 165836

90000

U.S. $8.95
Can. $11.95

SCHOLASTIC